A GIFT FOR:

PURCHASED FROM
MULTNOMAH COUNTY LIBRARY
TITLE WAVE BOOKSTORE

....

FROM:

....

Warm Wisdom

Insight and Inspiration

CATHERINE MARSHALL

J. COUNTRYMAN *Nashville, Tennessee*

CONTENTS

Adventure *7*

Beauty *9*

Bitternesss *10*

Blessing for New Home *11*

Books *12*

Career *14*

Christian Fellowship *16*

Citizenship *17*

Courtship *18*

Creativity *21*

Criticism *22*

Difficulties *24*

Discouragement *25*

Faith *26*

Family *29*

Forgiveness *32*

Generosity *34*

God's Gifts *35*

God's Love *37*

God's Patience *40*

God's Power *41*

God's Word *44*

Good and Evil *47*

Government *48*

Grief *50*

Guidance *52*

Guilt *54*

Habits *54*

Happiness 55

Heaven 57

Hopes and Dreams 58

Joy 60

Judging Others 61

Life 62

Life After Death 63

Marriage 64

Mediocrity 68

Meditation 69

Mistakes 70

Nature 71

Obeying God 73

Parenting 77

Peer Pressure 81

Praise 81

Prayer 82

Relationships 89

Remarriage 94

Rights 95

Romance 97

Self-Pity 99

Self-Will 100

Self-Worth 102

Sex 102

Sin 103

Single Parenting 104

Spiritual Qualities 106

Thoughts 106

Tithing 107

Traditions 109

Trusting God 110

Unsaved Loved Ones 112

Weddings 114

Women's Rights 116

Worry 117

Writing 119

Life is of the Heart as
well as the Head.

In spite of the homesickness,
I felt elation about being turned loose
to make my own way in the world. . . .
Not even father's disapproval
of teaching school in a place like
Cutter Gap had lessened
my enthusiasm. After all,
those other men and women down
through the centuries who had
accomplished things must have had to
shrug off other people's opinions too.

CHRISTY

ADVENTURE

If you want a humdrum . . . life, . . . try living without God, trying to manage your own affairs. But if you want real adventure, a zest for living, then give yourself—everything you have and are, every talent, your present and your future—away to Jesus Christ.

"Taste and see that the Lord is good"—I challenge you to try it for yourself!

The adventure of living has not really begun until we begin to stand on our faith legs and claim—for ourselves, for our homes, for the rearing of our children, for our health problems, for our business affairs, and for our world—the resources of our God.

BEAUTY

Mother had always
insisted that disorder and
dowdiness did
not glorify God or help
His cause one bit.

CHRISTY

BITTERNESS

"Bitterness is like a weed with a strong
root growing is us ... soon it will take
over the heart and contaminate us,
mind and spirit and body.
But that does not have to happen.
We can trust our Friend. He will root
out the bitterness and fill up the hole
where the root came out with
His love—if we will let Him."

MISS ALICE IN CHRISTY

Blessing for New Home

Lord, we ask Your blessing on this place. Cleanse it of any spirit of darkness or unhappiness that remains from those who lived here before. As we stand at the entrance, symbolically we take a branch of hyssop, dip it in the blood of the lamb, and touch the lintel and door posts as did the Israelites of Old Testament times when they wanted to protect their homes from plagues and evil spirits. As we go from room to room, we ask You in the Name of Jesus to fill each one with Your love, Your joy, and Your peace so that God's Spirit reigns in this place.

Books

Books are like friends. We must treat them like friends.

The real experiences of real people will forever remain the most fascinating, as well as the most helpful reading. That is doubly true when those real-life experiences help to answer the questions people most want answered these days—"How can I find God?"

Reading is so important in the making of mature, effective Christians. All of us should be knowledgeable about religious books, both for our own benefit and in order to guide others.

Career

God means that every career should be full-time service for Him. Dividing life into sharp compartments of the sacred and the secular is not God's doing. He needs consecrated lawyers, physicians, laborers, schoolteachers, politicians, housewives, and bus drivers as much as He needs ministers. So evaluate your unique bents and talents before making any final decision. . . . And don't underestimate how truly Christian almost any career can be.

Surely one of the tragedies of our time is that a highly industrialized, technological, and urbanized society has robbed millions of deep vocational satisfaction. God means for us to find the task that gives us the most joy to do. Then His plan is that monetary reward should come to us purely as a dividend.

When we . . . pick our jobs primarily for the material rewards, something devastating happens. Some shining quality goes out of work; it becomes drab and gray. Then we wonder why life holds so little excitement and why the things that we buy with our money give us limited satisfaction. We forget that "the chief end of man is to glorify God and to enjoy Him forever." And we forget that it's only as we seek to glorify God in our daily work that enjoyment of God and of life, even of ourselves is possible.

Women are deceiving themselves if they think the daily office grind is more glamorous and rewarding than being in the home.

Christian Fellowship

We must seek out mature Christian friends with whom we can share questions, problems, and the joys of discovery. Ideas will often come to our corporate mind that would not come to us in isolation. And sometimes God does speak directly through these friends. At the very least, their love, perspective, and common sense will help to steer us clear of wild tangents.

No Christian . . . ever gets beyond the need of wise counsel from other mature Christians.

Love for others has to be deep and genuine, if we are actually to be used to help them. Moreover, this love is not something that we can manufacture by an act of will. Love, like faith, is a gift of God.

CITIZENSHIP

Just occasionally it might be healthy for us to . . . go down on our knees in gratitude to God that we are citizens of the United States; being exceedingly grateful for the institutions and way of life that we have developed—including our higher education. We might even dust off our pride for a variety of seemingly inconsequential trivia—things like comfortable homes with central heating and attractive bathrooms; food of some variety and with some seasoning; salads; supermarkets; washing machines; plenty of paper and paper products.

COURTSHIP

I know of one girl who tried the following plan to find a husband. . . . She spent more money on clothes and make-up and more time on personal appearance. She tried joining organizations where there were men. . . . She read scores of self-help books. She enrolled in a modeling course that taught improved posture and social graces. She even toyed with the idea of moving to another section of the country where there would be a higher percentage of eligible men.

"This last I finally decided to skip," she laughingly told me. "All of this effort improved me, I'm sure. But in the end I seemed no closer to matrimony than before I started. Then I discovered the secret . . . It's simple enough, heaven knows. Actually I'd known it all the time . . . I'd been thinking of marriage in terms of what I'd get. As soon as I turned that round and thought of what I had to give someone else, my social life began to change. In the end it was my interest in my men friends—their thoughts, their problems, their needs that brought me love and marriage."

Peter Marshall was fond of reminding engaged couples that it was God who thought up love and romance in the first place. Marriage is an institution that He not only ordained, but has given His constant blessing. When we seek divine guidance in courtship and marriage, added blessings and happiness are the result. No wonder many a modern marriage is in jeopardy simply because two people have gone blindly on their way ignoring the Author of their love.

When Peter proposed, I wanted more than anything else to know God's will with certainty. I could not say "yes," without knowing that we had God's blessing. So, over dinner in a crowded tea room, Peter and I—quite oblivious to the people

around us—faced up to the question—would our fused lives and joint purposes be a greater asset to the world than if we went our separate ways? We sensed that real love should be an integrating force sending a couple on to greater success and greater victory in life than they could achieve singly. For even then I had a sense of destiny for Peter, and I had to be sure that I was supposed to be a part of that destiny.

The answer came a few days later. Both of us knew, with a sure inner knowing, that this—the loveliest thing either of us had ever experienced—was of God.

CREATIVITY

Creativity is the ability to put old material into new form. And it is only when old molds and old ways of doing things are forcibly broken up by need or suffering, compelling us to regroup, to rethink, to begin again, that the creative process starts to flow.

CRITICISM

The Greek word translated "criticize" in Moffatt, "Do not criticize at all" (1 Cor. 4:5), in King James is rendered "judge" or "judging." All through the Sermon on the Mount, Jesus sets Himself squarely against our seeing other people and life situations through this negative lens.

This Scripture seems to wrap it up for me:

So we do not criticize at all; the hour of reckoning has still to come, when the Lord will come to bring dark secrets to the light and to reveal life's inner aims and motives. Then each of us will get his need of praise from God.

1 CORINTHIANS 4:5 (MOFFATT)

1. A critical spirit focuses us on ourselves and makes us unhappy. We lose perspective and humor.

2. A critical spirit blocks the positive creative thoughts God longs to give us.

3. A critical spirit can prevent good relationships between individuals and often produces retaliatory criticism.

4. Criticism blocks the work of the Spirit of God: love, goodwill, mercy.

5. Whenever we see something genuinely wrong in people's behavior, rather than criticize them directly, or—far worse—gripe about them behind their back, we should ask the Spirit of God to do the correction needed.

DIFFICULTIES

When in a ticklish spot, I am to realize that I am there:

> By God's appointment
> In His keeping
> Under His training
> For His time

Regardless of what difficulties I am experiencing at the moment, or what things aren't as I would like them to be, I look at the circumstances and I pray, "What are You trying to teach me in these things? What do You want me to learn about this?" instead of making my first request, "Lord, change this for me."

Discouragement

Discouragement says, "My problem is bigger than God, who is not adequate to handle my particular need. So herewith I take my eyes off God, bow down before my problem, and give myself to it."

In digging through Scripture on this subject, I have discovered that no matter how difficult the situation, Jesus' attitude was always a calm, "Courage, My son, My daughter. Have no fear. There is nothing here that My Father cannot handle."

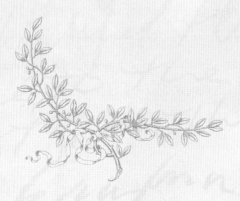

Faith

Hope must be in the future tense. Faith, to be faith, must always be in the present tense. Hope is the stepping-stone to faith, but only faith will forgive sins or heal.

Once we recognize our need for Jesus, then the building of our faith begins; . . . a daily, moment-by-moment life of absolute dependence upon Him for everything.

Have you ever asked God for the gift of faith? Or is this so obvious you've overlooked it? Be sure, however, that you really want what you ask for. Praying can be "dangerous business." If you ask for piano lessons, you'll have to do some practicing. If you ask for faith, you'll probably encounter situations immediately that will call for complete trust in God alone.

I have found no sure way to faith except that simple formula of handing one's will and one's self over to God.

Everyone has faith. The important question is: faith in what or in *whom*? In natural law? In science? In the government? In the power of evil? In one's own powers? Or in God?

God does not require faith of us as a sort of coin or passport to heaven's treasures. Faith is for *our* benefit. It's the bridge to the blessings of God.

FAMILY

God placed the solitary in families as one of the primary units in the Kingdom of God. If we will allow Him to be Lord of our lives, He will work out our problems for us. The family unit is His first proving ground, the school where He wants to demonstrate the riches He can pour into our lives and how His laws work in everyday life. He will use the very problems we face in the family as the exact vitamins necessary for our growth into mature spirits.

Depending upon our individual position in the family unit, God asks of us obedience and responsibility in a chain of Divine Order, which He has established. The husband is under Christ's authority; . . . the wife is the helpmate to the husband; . . .and children are to obey their parents "in everything, for this pleases the Lord."

The family is the training ground—the testing center—where sinners get on with the painful process of being pummeled into saints. I fear that God is not half so concerned with our being what we call "happy" in this life as in our being hammered and chiseled and molded into the characters He meant us to be all along.

And what is the most sure-fire method of rubbing off rough edges, forging us, shaping and molding us? Yes, you guessed. Parents rubbing against children; children bowing the will to parental authority as training for that bowing to God's authority.

The most cherished gift we parents can give our children . . . is our time—ourselves. No gift, no matter how expensive, can take the place of this.

If we make our faith a natural part of the home and share Christ in all aspects of family life, the children should be open to it naturally by adolescence, the point at which they are capable of rational decision-making. But if we've skipped our day-to-day homework and then try to introduce what is really a foreign concept to the child, it's going to be hard.

Perhaps our grandmothers knew a secret that women of this century need to rediscover. Because they thought of the guidance and development of their families as the most important thing in the world, homemaking turned out to be a big adventure rather than a chore. Precisely the same principle holds for the business world or community life or church work. How can even an ordinary person be jaded with life when extraordinary things are happening through her?

FORGIVENESS

Forgiveness has two sides that are inseparably joined: the forgiveness each of us needs from God, and the forgiveness we owe to other human beings.

Dislike and hate are emotions. We do not have complete control over ourselves at an emotional level. But we can tell God that we are willing to forgive—that our wills give full assent to what God wants, and ask Him to deal with emotion. When we are sincere in praying this we find sooner or later our intense feelings are just dissolved by God.

We need the healing forgiveness of Jesus Christ. He alone can sweeten sordid memories and take the sting out of deep hurts. We get that cleansing by going to Him and telling Him everything.

*True forgiveness
includes total acceptance.
And out of
acceptance wounds are healed
and happiness is
possible again.*

CHRISTY

GENEROSITY

Generosity of spirit is catching in a heart-lifting way, exactly as ill-humor is catching and has a depressant effect. Generosity of spirit has a way of dissolving seemingly immovable obstacles.

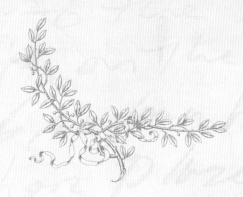

GOD'S GIFTS

All of God's good gifts are given by pure grace.

The God who made giraffes, . . . and a young girl's giggle has a sense of humor. Make no mistake about that!

Since we are His children and all the world's riches belong to the King, it follows that He can and will take care of our physical needs.

God is always far more willing to give us good things than we are anxious to have them.

*"God has all kinds of
riches for all of us.
Not just spiritual riches either.
His promises in the Bible are
His way of telling us what's available.
But this plenty doesn't become ours
until we drive in our stake on
a particular promise and
thus indicate that we
accept that gift."*

MISS ALICE IN *CHRISTY*

GOD'S LOVE

It is God's nature to love us. Nothing we can do or fail to do can stop the shining of that great love. Our misdeeds often make us turn our backs on God's love. In that case, we have left Him; He has not left us. He is still there loving us, yearning over us.

God is love, so He will not tell us to do anything unloving. God cares about other people as much as about us, so He will not tell us to do something selfish or harmful to others. His true guidance works for the benefit of all persons concerned. God is righteous, so He will not guide us to any impure act or dishonest act.

God's love is not affected either in quality or in extent by our actions.

*[God] persists
in receiving us and loving us
all even when we reject Him
and refuse to have
anything to do with Him,
even when we strut our little
intellects and insist that
He does not exist.*

CHRISTY

God's love is free of . . . ego and selfishness. There are times when He does say "no" to us. He is willing to run the risk of us misunderstanding, and is always disciplined; hence His is a powerful love.

God would not have bothered to create father-love and mother-love in the first place, if He Himself did not have it in great abundance.

God's love for us is so individual, Jesus told us He even has the hairs of our head numbered. Well, since that's true, surely He knows every little thing about each one of us and wants us to ask for His help with every little thing. But He does insist that we ask.

GOD'S PATIENCE

Often it seems to us that God moves slowly; that He refuses to accept the mad pace of our century.

As God works with each human life, His attitude is that of the artist who is creating a masterpiece—not just for time—but for eternity. No positive value ever built into any human personality is wasted. Therefore, God can afford to take infinite, painstaking trouble with each of us. He can be just as patient in molding us according to His perfect pattern, as we force Him to be. God is very patient.

One of the attributes of God is that He seems so leisurely. Have you noticed that? He seems to have the viewpoint of all eternity. Somehow we still haven't succeeded in persuading Him to accept the speeded-up tempo of our lives.

GOD'S POWER

Faith in God's power is at the heart of Christianity. Nothing else really matters but the question of all questions: Can you and I trust the love and the power of our God?

Thus an omnipotent God could make even "the wrath of man to praise Him." He can take any sins, any evil, any calamity— no matter where it originated—and make it "work together for good to them that love God."

The consistent voice of the sovereign power of God reverberates throughout Old Testament and New. He is the God of the supernatural—omnipotent, omnipresent, omniscient in this life and the next.

One day my mother and I stood at a window watching the fury of a thunderstorm of near-hurricane strength. It seemed drama on a cosmic scale—the clash of cymbals in the sky, the rolling of drums, fireworks of lightning. Rather than being afraid, I felt like shouting and applauding as the ferocious wind shook the great trees backward and forward as though they had been twigs clenched in the jaws of a dog. All the while, my mother's arm lay protectively around my shoulders.

Only in retrospect would I one day see the connection between these childhood experiences and my understanding of the nature of God. Then I would know that it made no sense at all that God would create my parents with a greater capacity for loving than He has Himself.

We should have a healthy fear of making our God too small.

GOD'S WORD

The Scriptures are the fascinating story of the directions God gave men and women; how guidance worked for them when they obeyed the instructions; what happened when they disobeyed.

Before you start to read any portion of the Scripture, breathe an inward prayer asking the Holy Spirit to open your mind and anoint your understanding of the passages. This should not be a ritual, but an adventure of faith as well as an experiment in prayer.

Start reading the Bible . . . to get to know God for yourself. . . . Get in the habit of reading a little bit of it the first thing in the morning or the last thing at night. Mark it up. Underline the places that seem to mean something special to you.

The New Testament contains surprisingly specific guidance for us. Its wisdom has the sure touch of ultimate truth. It is really a primer on the techniques of happy, workable relationships with other people. And that, after all, is the biggest single problem for any of us. We ignore these directions, therefore, to our own sorrow and loss.

Last week I produced a "Vitamin Box" of dozens of favorite passages for my new family. I used a concordance and looked up words such as strength, food, bread, water, hunger, and thirst. Other cards were culled from Christ's own words. Now before blessing the food at each meal, we pass the box, and one of the children chooses a card to read aloud. The nourishment is most effective when the life-giving words of Scripture are memorized and so become the permanent possessions of mind and heart.

*"God is the
living Alchemist who
can take the dregs from the
slag-heaps of life—disappointment,
frustration, sorrow, disease, death,
economic loss, heartache—
and transform the dregs
into gold."*

MISS ALICE IN *CHRISTY*

Good and Evil

The Bible story of the conflict between good and evil is not downbeat at all, but upbeat. It's the story of the total defeat of evil because of the absolute power of Christ.

An omnipotent God could make "even the wrath of man to praise Him." He can take any sins, any evil, any calamity—no matter where it originated—and make it "work together for good to them that love God."

Satan's strongholds are delusions, unreal, lies. . . . The only real stronghold is Jesus Himself and the truth He stands for.

GOVERNMENT

I believe strongly in the visioning prayer for leaders—the kind where we picture specific leaders growing in stature and maturity as they submit ambition and self to God's guidance.

My prayers for world leadership [are] twofold: that our current leaders will open themselves for God's guidance—and that in the future God will inspire and direct the right people into positions of leadership.

So Jesus' provision to save us and our nation is plain—a concerned minority dedicated to Him, who are willing to grasp firmly the handle of intercessory prayer in these critically dangerous days.

"If we're going
to work on God's side, we have
to decide to open our hearts to
the grief and pain all around us.
It's not an easy decision.
A dangerous one too. And a tiny
narrow door to enter into
a whole new world."

MISS ALICE IN CHRISTY

GRIEF

God's way of binding up our broken hearts will be to give us worthwhile work to do in the world.

Grief carries with it a strange phenomenon. Despite its universality, when sorrow comes to us, each of us is certain that no one has ever suffered such a keen sense of loss. And it is at that point that we can allow a poisonous self-pity to enter.

Grief is a wound—a very real wound—in the human spirit. The remedy must therefore be in that unseen, but very real world of the spirit. First of all, one has to face up to the situation as it is—not as one wishes it might be. Again and again, we must force ourselves to face sharp reality. This process is like iodine in an open wound. It stings temporarily, but it is the beginning of the whole healing process.

Mary Allen rocked
soundlessly on her heels,
grappling with the stark alternative
the doctor had handed her.

Yet no whimper escaped
her tight-set lips. Watching her,
I felt a great compassion and thought
how the grief of the inarticulate cuts
so much deeper than the loud wailing
of the self-pitying.

CHRISTY

Guidance

When we allow the Spirit to guide us He will concern Himself with our every desire and need.

God's voice will never contradict itself. That is, He will not give us direction through the inner voice of the Spirit that will ever contradict His voice in the Scriptures.

Watch the timing on guidance. If a strong inner suggestion is from God, it will strengthen with the passing of time. If not from Him, in a few days or weeks it will probably just evaporate.

When we have asked God to guide us, we have to accept by faith the fact that He is doing so. This means that when He closes a door in our faces, then we do well not to try to crash that door.

When we learn to listen to Christ's voice for the daily decisions we begin to know Him personally.

When we put our lives into God's hands and ask Him to direct us, amazing results will follow.

If you are standing at a crossroads (and life is full of crossroads), and you have asked God to tell you whether you are supposed to go down road A or road B, you have to be *willing* to go down either A or B. If you have asked and asked and don't get an answer, it is probably because you have set your heart on going down say, Road A, and don't *want* to go down B.

Obey God one step at a time, then the next step will come into view.

Guilt

God's wish is that no matter what we've done, we feel guilt only long enough to bring it to [Jesus], the Light of the World, to be dealt with.

Habits

We are creatures of habit patterns for good or ill. In other words, we do not make a series of equal and independent decisions, rather one decision leads to another.

Unfortunately, the natural inclination we have inherited from our father Adam toward making the wrong choice means that this phenomenon works more easily downward than upward.

Happiness

God's every thought, purpose, and plan since the beginning of time has been for His children's welfare and happiness.

All human unhappiness stems from but two roots:
1. misunderstanding and misinformation about God, and
2. failure to obey God.

I have observed that when any of us embarks on the pursuit of happiness for ourselves, it eludes us. Often I've asked myself why. It must be because happiness comes to us only as a dividend. When we become absorbed in something demanding and worthwhile above and beyond ourselves, happiness seems to be there as a by-product of the self-giving.

The God I know sometimes asks difficult things of us, it is true. But His will also includes a happiness here on earth abundant enough to float every difficulty.

God has designed us for happiness. He has created us for peace and joy.

HEAVEN

One thing I am sure of is that we cannot view heaven from our earthly limitations. For example, there will be no "time" in heaven, therefore no past, present or future, as we have on earth. In exactly the same way, I think that we will find distances completely different from what we know on earth.

HOPES AND DREAMS

All the resources of the universe leap to the help of those who dare to dream big.

Having discovered what you really want, give yourself fully to making that dream come true.

If Christ is in it, it pays to live dangerously.

Once you are sure that your dream is right, dedicating yourself completely to it necessarily involves a clear-cut decision of your will. It also means pledging an unstinting, joyous and lavish giving of all your time, effort, and talent.

God wants us to catch from Him some of His vision for us.

*"One of our tasks here
is to show folks a God who
wants to give them joy.
How they need joy!"*

MISS HENDERSON IN *CHRISTY*

JOY

What God wants for us is exactly what every thoughtful parents wants for his child—the pure, deep-flowing joy that springs out of maturity and fulfillment.

Christ still asks for the total surrender and then promises His gift of full, overflowing joy.

God allows us to have disappointments, frustrations, or even worse because He wants us to see that our joy is not in such worldly pleasures as success or money or popularity or health or sex or even in a miracle-working faith. Our joy is in the fact that we have a relationship with God.

Judging Others

Judging others constantly cultivates more soil for the thistles of fear-of-man to grow in.

Judgmentalism is an attempt to ward off the fear of criticism by standing in a superior place. Self thinks that when it can get there first and judge before others can state their opinions, it can forestall others' criticisms. Of course, self is mistaken, since the very opposite happens—judging draws the judgment of others.

LIFE

Each of us has a limited
number of years. So are we going to
go through those so-few years with
little time for our family and friends,
with unseeing eyes for the beauties
around us, concentrating on
accumulating money and things
when we have to leave them
all behind anyway?

CHRISTY

LIFE AFTER DEATH

In the next life I believe we will meet and know our relatives and loved ones as exactly who they are in relation to us, and we will have love for them we had on earth except that this love will have all selfish aspects or negative aspects taken out of it.

The evidence of Scripture, plus what Jesus Himself told us, . . . substantiate that there is no lag time at all between this life and the next. I believe we step right over the line at the point of death into the next world. Jesus' words to the thief dying beside Him on the Cross, "Today you will be with me in Paradise" would make no sense at all were there any cessation of the true life of the spirit—the real us between this life and the next.

Marriage

God wants every Christian marriage to be the most powerful twosome there can possibly be in this life. That unity has to be not just physical or even intellectual but a genuine spiritual partnership. True Christian marriage is really a threesome, because Christ is always included.

God is at the apex of the marriage triangle; the husband and wife are equally positioned at the lower corners. Thus both mates are equal in His sight, equally beloved by Him, equally committed to each other and to Him.

To develop the principle of wholeheartedness in marriage . . . , *go the second mile in the little, everyday things.* Life demands this, because our lives are merely the totality of countless little things.

It seemed to me that these child marriages were no good, that the girls caught in them never had a chance. . . . They were rushing at the pretense of being grown up when they were scarcely out of childhood, they could bring so little to the marriage. As Granny Barclay had once commented, "Green apples don't have much flavor."

CHRISTY

The wife is the helpmate to the husband, protected by him from stresses outside the home and even from any abuse from their children. God would elevate woman, not plunge her into servitude. Rather, her husband is to honor her with an unselfish love even as "Christ loved the Church and gave Himself up for her" (1 Peter 3:1–7).

The price of real success in marriage, as in any other career, is to give oneself to it fully. A divided self results in mediocrity.

God is supremely concerned about our happiness—yours and mine. But in His wisdom He knows . . . that self-centered people are never happy people. So in ordaining and blessing marriage, God certainly knew He was creating the world's best climate for character development. Intimate daily living with another human forces us out of our little self-centered world.

MEDIOCRITY

*A Christian has
no business being satisfied
with mediocrity. He's supposed
to reach for the stars. Why not?
He's not on his own anymore.
He has God's help now.*

CHRISTY

MEDITATION

Set aside a little time each day when you can get off by yourself and be quiet—quietness is essential. The powers of Hell just adore noise, you know. In the end, they hope to make this old world one great big pulsating racket.

Most people find early morning by far the best time. Get a notebook and pencil just for this purpose and keep them handy. Ask God for your marching orders for the day. Ask Him to invade your thoughts with His thoughts. Write down the thoughts that come to you.

Mistakes

Our God is the only One who can take life's rubbish heap—
our mistakes, disappointments, disobedience, and sin—and
through divine alchemy, make even these "to work together
for good." If this were not true, the gospel would be for the
angels, not for us imperfect creatures still walking the
warm earth.

No wrong turning is irretrievable. That's why the gospel
is Good News.

Nature

It was Jesus' custom to rise before dawn and slip outdoors to pray. A hillside or lakeside was His favorite spot for teaching (Matt. 13:1–2). A boat pushed out from the shore made a perfect pulpit (Mark 4:1). An olive grove in the Garden of Gethsemane was a favorite spot.

God's handiwork in nature fed and refreshed Christ's spirit. (Mark 6:46–47) . . .

Jaded by noise, jostled by people, harassed by things, we who live in the twenty-first century need to ponder and follow Jesus' example. We, too, need to slip away to be refreshed in the quietness and beauty of God's great outdoors.

*I do not know why it is
that an intimate contact with wildlife
and a personal observation of nature
helps so much in . . . self-discovery. . . .
Perhaps it is just that even a small city
provides artificial distractions that
separate us from the roots of our life;
even a few bricks and a little macadam
are a shield between us and the
wisdom that nature has to give.*

CHRISTY

Obeying God

The only way I will keep a pliable, obedient spirit in the larger decisions, is to look to God and *obey* Him in the smaller ones.

The point of this act of turning one's life over to God is that He will not violate the free will He has given us. And He cannot possibly lead someone who purports to be willing to obey Him one moment and like a balky mule, insists on his own way at the next moment.

It is not enough . . . to experiment with being obedient to God. It has to be a total decision in one's will.

If we were truly acquainted with the Father, we would count obedience to Him our greatest privilege.

Always and always the understanding comes after the obedience.

There are several ways of testing the guidance that comes to you. God is love, so He won't tell you to do anything unloving or selfish that would harm anyone else. God is righteous, so He won't ask you to do anything impure. Nor will He tell you to do anything contradictory to what He says in the Bible, because that's His voice too, and He cannot contradict Himself.

*"The only time
I ever find my dealings
with God
less than clear-cut is when
I'm not being honest with Him.
The fuzziness is always
on my side, not His."*

Miss Alice in Christy

Parenting

Rearing children and bringing them up "in the nurture and admonition of the Lord" is not only a full-time responsibility of any parent but is also the greatest witnessing field and mission field in the world.

There's no question, scripturally, that the man is to be the prophet, priest and king, so to speak, of his household. And the woman is to provide the support, the nurture.

It doesn't matter how prepared or unprepared the father is to become the head of the spiritual home. If he wades in and tackles it, he gets the help from God he needs. And the children get the right message, no matter now inarticulate the father may be.

There is only one road to the fine character we yearn for our children to have. That is to introduce them to Jesus Christ.

Parents need to be aware of some critical times in their child's development. For example, the first gift a child brings the parent is very, very important. It may be merely a weed from the lawn or a pretty rock, but when he offers that to the parent, the parent had better drop whatever he or she is doing, exclaim over it and accept it with great love. Too often we don't realize the importance of these seemingly little things until the children are grown and gone.

I had a father who gave us time—one of the hardest and most important things about parenting. It takes a lot of unselfishness.

"There is only
one way to give advice to
the young: give it, and then
be perfectly unconcerned as to
whether they take it or not.
God alone is capable
of managing other people—
even our own children."

MISS ALICE IN CHRISTY

Jesus is the only person who has the right to be put on a pedestal. If we climb down off the pedestal and are real, we can save our children a lot of heartbreak and disillusionment. Put yourself on a pedestal in the home and you invite tragedy. But when parents are transparent, they set the right example. The child should see a pattern of openness, confession, and immediate seeking of forgiveness from the Lord.

Sometimes as parents we grant our children their way, just because we lack the necessary discipline to say "no." This is really refined parental selfishness. We cannot bear for our children to doubt our love for them—even temporarily. This would impinge our ego. Our desire for the goodwill of our child is greater than the quality of our love, greater even than our determination to do the highest things.

Peer Pressure

Why is it obnoxious to God that we make the approval of our peer group the criterion of our conduct? The answer I receive is that when we make our decisions this way, *self* is at the center of our life instead of God.

Praise

Praise is faith in action, faith in its most vigorous form. When we praise:

- We are letting self go by turning our backs (an act of will) on the problem of grief where self has been most involved.
- We stop fighting the evil or less-than-good circumstances.
- With that, resentment goes; self pity goes.
- Perspective comes.
- We have turned our back on the problem and are looking steadily at God.

PRAYER

Talk it over with the Father, then leave the outcome to
His wisdom.

I know of no discipline in all the world like the discipline of
waiting on God. Rushing to conferences, rushing anywhere is
child's play compared to this. Faith is a living command. It can
be dangerous. It is costly. It is dangerous business because it
means putting ourselves at God's disposal, and sometimes
drastic changes have to be made in us before God can use us.

When an impossible situation confronts us we can pray,
knowing that to Jesus nothing is impossible.

The devil considers any real prayer dangerous.

*True prayer
can be rooted only in
the recognition of
genuine need.*

CHRISTY

To Jesus, prayer was the greatest adventure of His life. . . . In prayer He was stepping into the Presence of the Most-High God. . . . Sometimes Jesus spent the entire night in prayer with His Father.

I don't think Jesus wants us to use formal language. Talk to Him simply as a friend and Lord. Be honest. Admit your faults. Tell Him about your needs and hopes and dreams. Then ask for His help.

When you tell God that you will take either all or nothing, you are dictating your terms to Him and not leaving yourself open to His way of working out the problem. I have found over and over that His answers to prayer are often far different that what I expect or ask for, or even want.

Part of our problem in praying for our children, is the time lag, the necessary slow maturation of our prayers. But that's the way of God's rhythm in nature. For instance, the hen must patiently sit on her eggs to incubate them before the baby chicks hatch.

With this picture in mind, Dr. Glenn Clark suggests that we parents spend some time each day for at least a week thinking through our hearts' deepest desires for our children. After listing them on paper, ask for Jesus' mind on them, sifting out everything superficial or selfish until we have reached the kernel of the Spirit's hopes and dreams for this person.

Then copy these hopes in the form of prayers onto slips of paper cut in the shape of eggs and insert them between the pages of some favorite Bible—signifying leaving them in God's keeping.

In the persistent prayer—another name for it is the "waiting prayer"—it is not possible to make any rules. God is going to answer us through the Holy Spirit when it pleases Him to do so, and at that point that He deems the best timing. A memorable example of this is George Mueller's prayer for the salvation of five people. Mueller began praying for this fivesome in 1844 and continued the prayer for the next 54 years until he died, by which time three of the five had accepted the Lord. The last two did so after Mueller's death.

When we find ourselves deeply concerned for anyone, we should immediately lift that person in prayer to God. Imagine that person as helpless as a little baby, resting in your arms, unable to do anything for himself. Then, in an act of total dedication, gently, with a heart full of love offer that person up to God, who reaches out and takes him from our arms and into His own bosom. There is no safer place to be.

When we ask for God's help only in the major decisions, we are admitting Him into a very small part of our lives.

A demanding spirit, with self-will as its rudder, blocks prayer. . . . The reason for this is that God absolutely refuses to violate our free will. Therefore, unless self-will is voluntarily given up, even God cannot move to answer prayer.

There are various reasons why Jesus practiced secret prayer and asked us to follow His example. In our room with the door shut, we are not so likely to strut and pose and pretend as we are when another human being is present. We know that we cannot deceive God. Transparent honesty before Him is easier for us in isolation.

Relationships

A woman's true satisfactions have always been rooted in relationships rather than in accomplishment. That is why love is so necessary to our happiness. Always we've gotten more delight from people than from abstract ideas. Always we're looking for the human interest story behind the façade.

The bonds that unite families and friends are not forged for a little while, they are for eternity. They stretch across every boundary of space and time. They twine and intertwine from one generation to another, weave and interweave, priceless beyond measure.

Thinking first of the other person is the first step to love. But one cannot feign interest in other people; when it is artificial, it fools nobody.

*"No difference in
viewpoint should ever be
allowed to cause the least break
in love. Indeed, it cannot,
if it's real love."*

MISS ALICE IN CHRISTY

The Kingdom of God is the kingdom of right relationships.
That's what matters to Him.

Behind our broken human relationships, often lies one major
break—between God and us. We do not always recognize this,
being inclined to blame any dislocation in our lives on other
people, or on "circumstances," and to look for the remedy
anywhere but in a reconciliation with God.

I watch so many women seeking self-fulfillment in an office
only to find that office relationships can be just as difficult as
relationships in the home. Both need precisely the lubricant
Jesus teaches us to use—giving of ourselves to others. That
has to do with the inner spirit and our emotions. He alone
is Master there.

The single most important element in any human relationship is real honesty—with oneself, with God, and with others.

Our debt to the Heavenly Father is inordinate, unpayable, so we are at the mercy of the Father's compassion. In comparison with our debt to Him, the most any human being can owe another is trifling.

Our relationship with other people is of primary importance to God. Because God is love, He cannot tolerate any unforgiveness or hardness in us towards any individual. God commands that we forgive regardless who is to blame.

"No Christian ever has
a right to sever any relationship
with anybody out of anger or pique,
or even injustice, no matter how much
he disapproves of someone's actions.
It's our place to demonstrate
reconciliation—not judgment or
revenge or retaliation.
That's God's business, not ours."

MISS ALICE IN CHRISTY

REMARRIAGE

There is a danger, of course, that the lonely person will think that remarriage will immediately, automatically mend the hurt and solve all problems. Only a whole person is in a position to contribute to a marriage. The one who marries again out of blind need, and brings but half a person to the union, will find chances of a successful remarriage sorrowfully slim.

When the heart's motive is right, God will see that the result comes out right.

Rights

"All men are . . . endowed by their Creator with certain unalienable rights, (and) among these are life, liberty and the pursuit of happiness."

Now, I have always had immense admiration for Thomas Jefferson, author of these words. And until recently I never questioned them. But (and my apologies to you, Mr. Jefferson) I do question them as I see more and more people interpret "the pursuit of happiness" as a license to grab for power or money or physical pleasure.

The truth, as I see it, is that not one of us has "an unalienable right" to anything, not even to life itself. We did nothing to bring about our birth, and we are dependent for the next breath we draw on the grace of God. How arrogant and ungrateful we must seem to our Creator when we demand our "rights."

ROMANCE

When we truly love someone, our focus is on *him* or *her,* not on ourselves. And our constant thought is, "What can I do to give this beloved person joy? To please him? To ease his path? To minister to him?"

I do not think that the right way to pray about a husband is to figure out ahead of time what he should be like or what his role should be. I think you need to feel in your heart a very great desire for romance and love and then proceed by asking God to show you the internal spiritual qualifications, and qualities of mind and spirit and character that God would want in your life's mate. Then ask Him in His own way and in His own time to bring this man into your life.

In the love stories
that I had read the hero always
poured out his heart to the maiden
and won her with eloquence
and passion. Secretly I had hoped
that the man of my dreams
would approach me like that.
Well, romance in books and in real
life was obviously not the same.

CHRISTY

SELF-PITY

Since self-pity is a sin, then clearly it has be to dealt with as a sin. A sin because since I belong to Jesus, it is He who has control over my life. Thus He overrules everything that He "allows" to happen to me—overrules it for *good*.

My part is to trust Him as a loving Heavenly Father in each of these adverse circumstances. I am to watch expectantly for the "good". . . the new adventure He has for me . . . the open door I am to go through toward the better way to which He is leading me.

SELF-WILL

Whatever your problem is—whether it's fear or the seeming inability to believe or unforgiveness or grief—all your problems really resolve themselves into one problem: Is self still controlling your will, or are you willing to hand it over to God?

By giving humans freedom of will, the Creator has chosen to limit His own power. He risked the daring experiment of giving us the freedom to make good or bad decisions, to live decent or evil lives, because God does not want the forced obedience of slaves. Instead, He covets the voluntary love and obedience of children who love Him for Himself.

God has given you and me free will. And the voluntary giving up of our self-will always has a cross at the center of it. It is the hardest thing human beings are called on to do.

"The Creator
made the world a cooperative
enterprise. In order for it
to be that way, God had to give
us the privilege of going
His way or of refusing
to go His way."

MISS ALICE IN CHRISTY

Self-Worth

When I had progressed in my piano lessons far enough to play simple hymns, Father would sometimes allow me the fun of being the pianist in a small church parlor meeting.

Thus, early, I was given a sure sense of self-worth, the recognition of my individuality, and the surety of being loved and cherished. These are securities that parents can give their children only through their actions.

Sex

Satan cannot create anything new, cannot create anything at all. He must steal what God has created. Thus he twists love and God's wonderful gift of sex into lust and sadism and myriad perversions. He disfigures the heart's deep desire to worship God and persuades us to bow before lesser gods of lust or money or power.

SIN

Sin is largely a matter of mistaken priorities. Any sin in us that is cherished, hidden, and not confessed will cut the nerve center of our faith. A guilty conscience will inevitably produce fear—the antithesis of faith.

What shall we do with our sins? Be honest about them before God. Abandon them. Waste no time moaning about them. Accept forgiveness immediately—and our faith will flow back stronger than ever.

SINGLE-PARENTING

Single-parenting is a major factor in church and community life . . . and will be increasingly in this decade. The church must adapt.

⁓

We have to be very careful about the schools our children attend and the companions they have in their formative years.

⁓

Children from broken homes have memories that must be healed. Without healing, that generation will just breed up more hurt. Every child needs support form a father *and* a mother. Sometimes you have to relinquish your child to another influence. It's part of our spiritual protection that God often provides someone outside the family to be a major positive influence on your child at a key time in his life.

Every single parent needs a supportive Christian community. The Bible has a lot to say about caring for widows and orphans. And this, of course, involves the single parent.

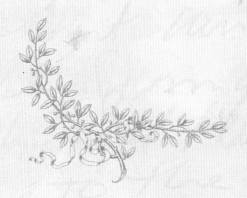

Spiritual Qualities

Not a single spiritual quality—faith, peace of mind, joy, patience, the ability to love the wretched and the unlovely—can we work up by self-effort. Anyone who has tried, knows that he cannot. . . . But . . . "with God all things are possible."

Thoughts

Our faith is built up and appropriated as we form habitual thought-patterns that accentuate the positive. Day after day our thoughts are either taking us toward life or toward death.

TITHING

I do not speak of tithing as a way to get rich quick! No, the amazing effect of my tithing experiment has been twofold: (1) It has completely freed me of the panic fear that used to grip me about being penniless. Now I know that my needs will always be supplied. And (2) it has helped me to know the joy of being a channel through which blessings can flow to those around me. The Lord's purse is never empty!

TRADITIONS

The act of doing things together in a family reaches deep inside a child and satisfies his thirst for community, for fellowship, for proof that he isn't alone in the world.

That's why traditions based on family activities give the individual security and strengthen family ties. The traditions return again and again to remind us of the imperishables that help make up the foundation of our lives—love of family, companionship, humor, enthusiasm, gratitude. Our life would not be worth living without these qualities. But every parent knows the difficulty of teaching them to our children, who are born self-centered. They can't see humor, or handle love, or touch gratitude. Yet love is every bit as real as granite, and gratitude is just as much a reality as fire, so these verities must be dramatized for our children . . . through the medium of family traditions.

Trusting God

Not one of us finds it easy to put our problems into God's hands completely. But only in that way does our trust in Him grow.

Y

If we cannot believe that God can help us recover from troubles shaped by human beings as well as those we bring upon ourselves, then we have a narrow basis indeed for our faith in Him.

Y

Only as we proceed to act out our trust, will the emotion of confident faith well up within us.

Y

We demonstrate trust by placing the thing or person or situation we are concerned about into the Father's hands to do with as He pleases. . . . This is faith in action.

God requires us to have faith in the fact that He really is an all-loving God in Whom there is no darkness and that He really does love us. It is only after we are willing to stand on that and deposit our trust in His love that we begin to get some answers.

When we make God's will, our will, our deepest happiness and welfare also glorifies God and extends His kingdom on earth. We can trust a God like that!

There comes a point in the matter of trusting God for a real need, when to continue to rely on Him alone seems terribly risky. A definite decision involving our wills then has to be made. Will we decide to stake everything on God, or will we turn back and try human resources?

Unsaved Loved Ones

No human being can sink too low for the Love and Light to rescue him, . . . and heavenly hosannas still ring out so loudly as almost to split the sky, as each lost and staying sheep is hauled back from the abyss of self-destruction.

Nagging won't accomplish anything. It takes a lot of praying. It means giving more, much more than is expected of you. It means going not just the second mile, but also the third— whatever it takes to help the non-believer understand God's love. . . . I believe the non-believer can be won over, but it may take many, many years. This is all part of that tensile strength the Lord gives us when we refuse to buckle under.

"Either God exists—

or He does not. If He does,

either an individual has a relationship

with Him or that relationship

has been severed."

MISS ALICE IN *CHRISTY*

WEDDINGS

We spend more money than the people of any other country for expensive and ultra-fashionable weddings and all the trappings of romance. And we find in the end that tons of orange blossoms, thousands of yards of tulle and lace, gallons of champagne, and all the right gestures and words, usually fail to give the desired result. For true romance lies deeper than materialism. It is the product of the depths of the human spirit. And that's where God comes in.

WOMEN'S RIGHTS

The emancipation of women really began with Christianity—when a girl—a very young girl—received the greatest honor in history. She was chosen to be the mother of the Savior of the world. And when her Son grew up and began to teach His way of life, He ushered women into a new place in human relations. He accorded woman a dignity she had never known before.

Women are emancipated in a hundred ways they didn't used to be. And that's good. But the tendency now is to give short shrift to homemaking and children. That's a key problem—children aren't getting enough time from their parents—mothers or fathers. And the problem is that the child will equate the love of God with how much real love he's getting from his parents.

WORRY

Living in the past or worrying about the future is what spoils the *now* for us. Either one keeps us from giving our full attention to the present.

WRITING

Life, as you and I know it, is of the heart as well as the head. Therefore, literature, if it is accurately to reflect life, must at times, reach past the reader's intellect to the emotional level. In order to achieve that, the writer has to *feel* something as she writes.

I spend much time trying to find the precise word that will convey what I'm trying to say. And almost always before I begin, I breathe my own little silent prayer that God will write through me. It is astonishing how this is answered. Somehow when you really mean this, He does achieve it, even in some of these wooden days when you don't feel all that inspired.

There is no basic training in writing like trying one's hand at poetry. In poetry one has to find the precise word. One's thoughts have to be placed in small compass—as sharp as an arrow. Imagination has to come into play, or the poetry is just—blah. And discipline—ah discipline!